She Wore Her Serenity Brightly

# She Wore Her Serenity Brightly

A Portrait of
Dorothy Robertson Aitken

Shoving Leopard

First published in 2006 by
Shoving Leopard Productions
8 Edina Street
Edinburgh EH7 5PN

info@shovingleopard.com
www.shovingleopard.com

ISBN 1 905565 00 3 paperback

Further copies are available from booksellers,
www.shovingleopard.com,
and M. J. Brown Son & Co, 10 Dean Bank Lane,
Edinburgh EH3 5BS

All profits from *She Wore Her Serenity Brightly* will be donated to The PathWay Charitable Trust.

Front Cover photograph: Dorothy as Queen Dido in the Edinburgh Opera Company's 1959 production of Dido and Aeneas. *Photo courtesy of The Evening Dispatch (The Scotsman Publications) supplied by Alexander (Alan) Brebner and used with permission.* Dido: Dorothy Robertson; Aeneas: Alan Brebner; Handmaiden: Jean Walker

Line drawings by: Helen Hutcheson
Cover design: Heather Macpherson

To the memory of a wonderful friend,
singer and teacher

**Dorothy Robertson Aitken**

22 October 1928 – 27 March 2005

# Contents

# Introduction

'Do not go where the path may lead, go instead where there is no path and leave a trail'

*Ralph Waldo Emerson, (1803 - 1882)*

This book is a wonderful way to celebrate the memory of my mother. She would have been surprised and proud at how fondly she was remembered and at how many people have felt moved to contribute. She has helped so many people to achieve their musical goals and I know many will be thinking of her for a long time to come. She will always be in our thoughts.

As any monies raised are being donated to the PathWay Charitable Trust.

I am going to take a few lines to explain about the Trust and why it was recently set up. This is a venture which Dorothy was keen to support and would have been happy to be remembered through.

The PathWay Trust has been set up to provide better ways of assessing people with various sorts of developmental problems. Autism, Aspergers' Syndrome and attention-deficit hyperactivity disorder are all conditions which were rarely diagnosed or recognised until the past decade, but are now commonplace. The work of the Trust will use methods which are innovative and have not yet become part of routine clinical practice.

The aim is to help people access therapies which are not otherwise available to them because of expense or lack of expertise.

*Dr Ken Aitken*
*Bruntsfield, September 2005*

The PathWay Charitable Trust
1 Wemyss Place
Edinburgh EH3 6DH

# Our friendship

Helen Murdoch has an M.A. in English literature from Glasgow University. She is a lecturer and theatre historian. Publications include: *Travelling Hopefully – a biography of Molly Urquhart*; musical plays (published by Samuel French) include: *Alan and the King's Daughter*, *A Dragon for Dinner*, and *Jenny and the Lucky Bags*, all with music by Ethel McCracken. Helen also contributed to the National Dictionary of Biography published in 2004.

The friendship I shared with Dorothy Robertson Aitken has been one of the most enriching of my life. To begin to describe her is almost an impossible task. I want to tell the story of our friendship, so to use a quotation that to me, conveys something of her personality, I have borrowed from James Thurber's wondrous fairy tale 'The Thirteen Clocks'. He says of the Princess:

'She wore her serenity brightly, like the rainbow'

And so did Dorothy.

I first saw her at a rehearsal of Verdi's Macbeth with the Glasgow Grand Opera Society in the YMCA hall in Bothwell Street, Glasgow. Neil Mundy, a well-known director of musical productions and Principal Science Teacher at Strathbungo Secondary School, had been invited to direct this production. Millar Hart, Head of Technical Subjects and myself, a humble assistant teacher of English were the teaching colleagues who helped him in the annual school Gilbert and Sullivan productions, so we were thrilled to be invited to help back stage on such an impressive venture.

The hall was thronged with singers making the splendid 'getting ready' noises prior to performances. They were going to begin with the famous Letter Scene and Aria where Lady Macbeth vows that she will help her husband to become King of Scotland by fair means or foul.

'Which is Lady M?' I whispered. Neil pointed to a pretty young blonde girl, talking and laughing with a group of friends.

'Surely not her!' I thought, looking around at several tall, dark-haired women of more menacing appearance.

The music began. Dorothy walked into position. She seemed to grow about six inches taller, her expression changed and she began to sing.

I was mesmerised. Her rich, soaring voice, her expressive intensity, her bearing all conveyed the fierce Lady of Glamis vividly, her dramatic skill imbuing every note, every syllable, with chilling resolve. There, in her every day clothes in a rehearsal space, Dorothy gave the performance of a great and gifted singer. I was thrilled to think I would be hearing her sing as the centrepiece of a strong supporting company for all the rehearsals as well as a week's performance in the splendid Alhambra Theatre.

Some parts of the libretto the company was using had phrases that were not easily sung and a few possessed that strange melodramatic turn typical of early 20th century libretti. I had written lyrics before, so Neil suggested to Dorothy that I might be able to help. She was charming and we became friends immediately; revamping such oddities as 'Get thee hence, audacious greybeard!' and 'Maledictions, maledictions come upon ye!' into more comprehensible and singable words!

During these times I met Dorothy frequently and began to learn how her musical career had begun. Her first performance on stage, she recalled, was when she was four years old. Dressed in blazer, cap and shorts, she appeared through the curtains of Glasgow's old Lyric Theatre, describing the feelings of an impatient small boy on a train journey to Fife. This, she declared, received tumultuous applause.

Her next public performance was at her piano teacher's annual concert when she would have been around thirteen. She had elected to play 'Rustle of Spring' by Sinding, from memory. She began in fine style, with those first thrilling eight bars. Her mother, sitting in the front row, looked up enquiringly when she played those eight bars again… and then again. She had forgotten what came next! Always the trouper, she'd repeated the phrase a generous dozen times. Having given the audience its money's worth, she got up and bowed in response to puzzled applause as her mother sat, hands over her face, rocking back and forth in acute embarrassment!

Dorothy in her teens was taking music lessons and her enthusiastic teacher was entering her in for Music festivals, often with her great friend, Mary Falconer. They came first on many occasions, but it is typical of Dorothy that she mostly related the amusing episodes.

Once for a church concert, they had been asked to include a duet at short notice just before the event. This meant that they were going to have to sing, unusually, from the music. At the rehearsal they found the small print too difficult to read in the stage lighting. Dorothy took five minutes to fix that. As they came to sing the number, Dorothy in the wings proudly displayed her solution. She had written the words out in a much larger print.

'You see,' she said to May, 'where the writing slants to the right, you sing that bit. If it slants to the left, I sing it. If my writing is straight up and down, we sing it together.'

They walked on stage. It was too much for May who burst out laughing. She stopped only to explain to the audience 'I want to tell you what my friend has just said…'

The audience roared with laughter. It was, Dorothy recalled proudly, the hit of the evening.

Once a young music teacher asked Dorothy to be the guest singer at his annual church choir concert. It was to be an ambitious programme presented in some style. Would she wear evening dress, he asked? He would pick her up an hour before.

As always she was impeccably prepared and dressed for the occasion, in a blue taffeta dress and silver slippers; with a little velvet jacket round her shoulders, she came down the garden path to greet her escort exactly on time. Jack Henry (who shall remain nameless!) presented her with a corsage, then balanced her on the bar of his bicycle and off they went in style!

Another famous incident in the history of the Glasgow Grand occurred when it was decided to stage Macbeth again, with Geoffrey Corbett conducting, again at the Alhambra Theatre.

There is a ballet in Verdi's version which the director had decided to include. He engaged young dancers, trained in Glasgow by the celebrated Katherine Marks, sister of Alice Marks (Alicia Markova). The chorus, male and female, awaiting the arrival of Macbeth to question the wise women about the fulfilment of the prophecy, were arranged around the stage in dark jewel coloured monks' cowls made by the wardrobe department out of rayon-type lining material. This promised to be a most effective scene and Dorothy, as Lady Macbeth, was waiting in the wings to see how the dress rehearsal performance would go. The theatre was full of friends and relations. As the scene progressed, a ripple of laughter came up from the audience which developed quickly to such a volume that they were soon rolling in mirth. The people on stage could not see what was causing this, so carried on manfully.

Without consulting the lighting experts, the director had included ultra violet light to create a special spectral effect. It did! It caused any white nylon material underneath the cowls to light up. A whole illustrated history of British underwear was on display as all lingerie from Spirella to Marks and Spencer shone in brilliant fluorescence – for one performance only.

Dorothy of course had played leads in the Glasgow Grand Opera Society from her late teens. She had an outstanding success as Marguerite in a rare revival of Boito's *Mefistofele*, playing alongside Richard Lewis and Ian Wallace, the celebrated baritone who spoke very highly of her performance. (His comments are recorded elsewhere in this anthology).

She also received critical acclaim for her portrayal of Abigaille in Verdi's *Nabucco*, when one critic praised her performance remarking on her 'splendidly sustained disdain'. The effect was achieved partly because her long jewelled earring caught on her equally bejewelled shoulder when she turned her head – she played the rest of the act looking disdainfully at anyone and everything on her left! Another illustration of Dorothy's endearing characteristic of laughing at herself! But her preparation and performance were always seriously and sincerely sustained.

Later, when she played the title role in *Lucia di Lammermoor*, her performance, said Robins Millar, the Daily Express critic, 'deserved to be classed alongside those of Maria Callas and Joan Sutherland'. I certainly remember weeping every night when she played that wonderful Mad Scene. A party from the German Consulate in Glasgow came on the first night, then booked for every subsequent performance.

Always on time for every cue, always totally in command of things, she did give us one scare. Just before the wedding ceremony, when the assembled guests await the unhappy young bride, forced into a loveless marriage by the brother who hopes thereby to restore the family fortunes, the sprightly music for the dance is suddenly hushed as the announcement of Lucia's imminent arrival silences the throng. Silence. The conductor's baton was poised, ready, the orchestra sat alert, the chorus grouped to see her arrival... What had gone wrong?

There is nothing so frightening in the middle of an opera than a sudden inexplicable silence. It was going on too long! I glanced around desperately. Dorothy was there in the wings doing a strange little dance.

'You're on!' I hissed.

She looked surprised.

'Two more pages' she whispered.

Her friend May Falconer slipped into the wings from her position in the chorus...

'Dorothy! It's you!'

She leapt forward. Veil and train adjusted, she flung the double doors open and glided on, a frail, unhappy desolate little bride who had, it seemed, been too terrified to take the final steps to her fate. What an actress!

Later, I asked her what had happened.

'One of the stagehands said to me, "You can do the twist to that music!" We were just giving it a try'.

The only time she nearly missed an entrance!

When Scottish Opera began, Alexander Gibson invited her to take part in the 'Opera for All' touring company. Because of home commitments, she went only part-time, having made fool-proof provision for husband John and small son Kenneth. He remembers the masses of pies and cakes prepared for their meals with some family support. The tours took her all over the country to the Highlands, Lowlands and several English dates. Dorothy always loved it. She said she had all the fun without the continuous daily performances, though no doubt she would have coped with those if necessary. The different audiences received the productions warmly and some linked TV coverage made the company well known.

There were anecdotes and stories never ending. One of my personal favourites happened, as Dorothy told it, when she was sitting having lunch in a Pitlochry hotel before her evening performance as Donna Anna in Mozart's *Don Giovanni*. An American, also a guest in the hotel, was impressed by her calm demeanour in view of the heavy role to be sung that evening.

'You are so calm, lady. Don't you have any butterflies?'

Dorothy considered for a moment.

'Well, not here. But I'll have one in the Borders and two in Manchester!'

Always ready to help, Dorothy agreed to take part in a musical entertainment I had devised for the senior pupils in my school. We called it, in Samuel Johnson's immortal phrase, 'Opera is an exotic and irrational entertainment'. This was to consist of several related readings from Shakespeare, Scott, Beaumarchais and other sources of libretti, matching these with the arias relating to them. Singing in a school double classroom with desks piled at one end to allow performing space, piano and seating, Dorothy sang, as always, perfectly and without reference to the music. The pupils read the passages chosen, and the audience was staff and fellow pupils. There were a great number of converts to opera that evening!

We repeated the idea at Hamilton College of Education, with full staging costumes and lighting by the gifted drama lecturer, the late Arthur Brittain. Dressed in what seemed like a Ralph Lauren gown in shimmering gold silk, Dorothy made a fantastic entrance, coming down a little staircase singing 'Love and Music' from *Tosca*. The effect was stunning, and students dragged there unwillingly by their mates stayed to applaud vociferously. The student groups sang wonderfully and the whole evening was one of those one-off memorable occasions. The dress? She had made it herself out of a taffeta type lining fabric – for £4!

A series of recitals for an American Scottish Summer School held at Carberry Towers allowed a further development of this idea. A group of singers including Dorothy, Joan Busby and Donald Maxwell sang a selection of scenes and music from *Cosi fan Tutte*. The fine pianist, Kathleen Belford, was accompanist and the reading framework of the evening, giving the story and highlighting the arias, that I had written, was given a fine performance by Ian Aldred from the BBC. I was privileged to write similar narrations for the Marriage of Figaro and for Puccini's *Manon Lescaut*. They were like mini, portable operas and were given several performances, some by Joan Busby at her long established summer school at Oxenford.

Dorothy really was the most engaging personality on and off stage. She loved to recite anecdotes and Kenneth's patient comment, when his mother was rehearsing 'There's that old Lady Macbeth yelling again!' has already been recorded. But it isn't generally known that the rather highly strung boxer dog named Macduff who had entertained the Aitken household for some time, would listen quietly and it seemed with great enjoyment to Dorothy singing. But should she sing Spanish songs such as those by Albeniz or de Falla, he would stand up and join in, howling enthusiastically if not very tunefully or rhythmically all the way through. This only happened with Spanish songs.

Then, our canary, an elderly bird resigned to bachelorhood, well fed and lively but silent for literally years, burst into song whenever I played a tape of

Dorothy singing Mozart's *Exultate Jubilate*. The whole range of classical music, singers, orchestras, he ignored. But that piece restored his youth.

So much to tell, as so many friends must have. Holidays, being swept into a champagne reception at the interval of the ballet in Budapest. We had been watching Bartok's *Magnificent Mandarin*. Looking for coffee in the interval, a door in the vestibule wall had swung open. Dorothy, looking radiant as ever, signed 'Could we come in?' She and I following were ushered inside, plied with food and drink and received rapturous appreciation when we said we came from Edinburgh. This was a reception apparently for important guests and foreign journalists. They were happy, we were happy. The young ballerina curtsied to Dorothy when she congratulated her. 'She think I'm someone special' whispered Dorothy – the dancer was right, she was!

What else? Glorious Scottish holidays, Dorothy occasionally singing in the car. On one notable occasion, she sang 'Lo here the gentle lark' to a positively glorious lark obbligato in Galloway. Laughing that heavenly laugh at Francie and Josie, yes and even Ken Dodd. Late supper after the many plays and musical evenings we had. A phone call late at night, saying 'It's only me…' If only! She gave us the glory of her music and the warmth of her friendship. We all have such wonderful memories. These we will have forever.

'She wore her serenity brightly…'

# Anecdotes and Tributes

All our talents increase in the using, and every faculty, both good and bad, strengthens by exercise.

Anne Brontë (1820-1849)

Quote given to Jane Butters by Dorothy

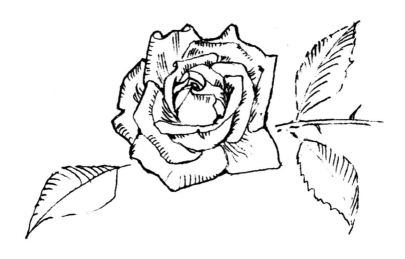

She made possible the impossible…

Dorothy was not only a truly gifted performer and teacher (though for most of us these achievements would be enough). She was an inspiration. Her character energised all those fortunate enough to know her, and made possible the impossible.

Garry Walker, pupil, conductor

I wish I could sing…

In 1994 at the end of a concert, I made a heartfelt but hardly noticeable comment about how I'd love to learn to sing. Two days later there was a note from Dorothy giving me details of a singing teacher (who after 6 weeks, moved 600 miles away!). I still can't really sing, but Dorothy's kindness stayed with me and my singing teacher friend and I still keep in touch after all these years.

Bless you, Dorothy.

Veronica Ashby, friend

Of course, I'm only 57...

The anecdotes are many, chiefly "of course I'm only 57." We knew this was not the case and I thought she was 70 last October. Dorothy treated us to supper on 19th February at La Piazza in Shandwick Place. We ended up with coffee at the Cally* and she glided elegantly in her golden raincoat to Frasers' to get a taxi and that was the last time I saw her.

Margaret Lang, pupil


*Caledonian Hotel*

Dorothy could sleep through an air raid...

My Mum, Dad, sister and I went to King's Park Glasgow (Dorothy's home) for a weekend holiday during the Second World War, 1941 I think. Dorothy and I had to sleep on the couch and chairs in the lounge. During one night there was an air raid and we were all wakened. We were taken to the air raid shelter at the bottom of the garden. As this part of Glasgow was very near a gun battery we could hear explosions etc. Quite a while into the raid it became clear that Dorothy was not amongst us! Her father ran back into the house – Dorothy was still fast asleep. After the raid we realised there were large pieces of shrapnel in the garden and on the roof of the house. If one of these had got in to the house – we would have had a quite another story!

Nancy Barr, née Robertson, cousin

Memories of a wonderful teacher…

Dorothy was a wonderful concert attender. She virtually never missed a performance, which, considering the vast number of her pupils, was a remarkable feat in itself.

In the audience she breathed every breath with you, and lived every phrase!

Afterwards she was encouraging and generous in her comments, and on several occasions gave me gifts to mark the show. Amongst these was a perfume called *Diva,* to which she certainly had a right, although I am sure I did not! When I played Carmen, she presented me with a brooch which had belonged to her mother, saying that she wanted me to have it, because her mother would very much have enjoyed my performance. Needless to say, it is in my box of treasures, and I was very glad to lend it to another of Dorothy's pupils as the *something borrowed* to be worn on her wedding day, which Dorothy also attended. I still have several pieces of costume which she gave me, and which she was delighted to see used again on stage.

Her knowledge of songs was encyclopaedic, and of great help to me in planning programmes. I am sure she was never able to keep track of the enormous piles of music she leant out to everyone! She was always delighted too to be introduced to a song she didn't know.

As a teacher she was absolutely to be trusted. I felt she would always be honest with me, whilst always encouraging me to take up new challenges and stretch the limits of what was possible. This honesty, coupled with immense kindness, made her comments and suggestions so much more valuable than mere praise would have been.

It was easy to overlook the considerable experience of performing at the highest level which Dorothy had enjoyed, before some of us knew her. Her modesty meant that she never showed off about roles she had played, or name dropped about the people she had worked with. Just occasionally,, when she wanted to make as suggestion as to interpretation or speed, one would get a glimpse of how things had been done by Harwood, or Geraint Evans, or Gibson, and realise just how good she must have been in her heyday. I would so much like to have seen her as *Butterfly*, or heard her *Frauenliebe und Leben*, which was one of the last things we worked intensely on together.

When I told my mother about her death, and was musing about how many people would miss her so much, my Mum, who met her several times, said, 'Ah yes, but you were one of her special ones, weren't you?' I wasn't - or at least, not any more special than any of her students. That gift for making you feel important to her was part of what made her unique.

Thank you, Dorothy, for everything.

Ann Heavens, singer, actor and director of Cameo

Her professional opinion…

I have fond memories of Dorothy. I was always delighted to bump into her at a Festival concert in the Usher Hall and eager to hear her professional opinion of the soprano or the tenor or whoever. The lovely thing about her was that she would always ask my opinion as well, and listen to my view (coming from a complete musical amateur) with genuine interest. She had a lovely way of making you feel included in her life even if our acquaintance was brief. And she had the most wonderful smile!

Laurence Hunter, friend

Dorothy was always very kind and encouraging. I enjoyed singing with her – it seems like yesterday!

Alexander (Alan) C. Brebner, friend

# Photographs – the early years

*Dorothy aged twenty months*

*Nancy and Dorothy, 1934 (supplied by Nancy Barr)*

*The happy little butterball...*

*Dorothy, Drew and their mother*

*In Mr Millay's choir' supplied by May Falconer, Dorothy's great friend.... the choir of King's Park Parish Church and Mr Millay, organist and wonderful choir master.*

*Dorothy with the choir…*

*Dorothy's parents' Silver Wedding, 1943*

*Dorothy and John's wedding*

**M**ISS DOROTHY ROBERTSON,
  *leading soprano of Glasgow Operatic
Society, and MR J. W. AITKEN, of
Ralston, after their wedding in King's Park
Church, Glasgow.*

*Dorothy and John on page 2 of the morning special edition of
The Sunday Post, Sunday April 27th 1952*

*A further wedding photo...*

*Dorothy and John in attendance...*

# The Singing Years – photographs and tributes

*Programme from the 1959 performance of Dido and Aeneas (see the cover photo) kindly supplied by Alexander (Alan) Brebner*

PURCELL TERCENTENARY

## The Edinburgh Opera Company

*Hon. Vice-Presidents :*
The Rt. Hon. The Earl of Dalkeith      Lady Steel-Maitland

will present

# DIDO and AENEAS

preceded by
the Choruses and Incidental Music
from
THAMOS, KING OF EGYPT
(Mozart)
in the
## GATEWAY, ELM ROW
for the week commencing
### MONDAY, 13th APRIL, 1959
at 7.30 p.m.

THE EDINBURGH CHAMBER ORCHESTRA
*(Leader : Jessie Veitch)*

*Musical Director* ................. Andrew Miller
*Producer* .......................... Cecil Hole
*Chorus Master* .................... Owen Connolly
*Ballet Mistress* ...................... June Geissler
*Wardrobe Mistress* ................ Cis Gilbert
*Stage Manager* .................... John Wilkie

*The Ballet sequences will be danced by*
*Pupils of the June Geissler School of Dancing*

*Solo Dancers :* June Geissler and Roy Muir

*56*

Principal Parts will be played by :

| | |
|---|---|
| DOROTHY ROBERTSON | JEAN WALKER |
| JANET PRENTICE | ALAN BREBNER |
| NAN RENNIE | MARY ELLIOT |
| LOTTIE SEGGIE | FLORA McLEAN |

CHORUS :

Jean Alexander, Janette Arrighi, Georgena Brews, Violet Byers, Jean Craig, Edith Duncan, Moira Fisher, Johan Hendry, Dorothy Johnstone, Rena Kelly, June Laidlaw, Joy McDowell, Margaret McIntosh, Katherine McQuarrie, Roberta Murray, Barbara Robertson, Irene Rowe, Mary Steven, Barbara Thomson.

Andrew Allan, Donald Ball, Owen Connolly, Mitchell Grieve, James Howat, George Johnstone, Neil McIvor, John Marshall, Tom Murray, John Paterson, Michael Rowe, John P. Small.

*Accompanist :* Kenneth McKenzie

*Chairman :* John Paterson

*Vice-Chairman :* John P. Small

*Hon. Secretary :* T. R. Michael Rowe,
13 Great Stuart Street, Edinburgh 3

*Hon. Treasurer :* James Steven
13 Polwarth Park, Edinburgh 11

---

### PRICES OF ADMISSION

| | | |
|---|---|---|
| Centre Stalls (Front and Rear) | ... | 5/- |
| Side Stalls (Rear) | ... ... ... | 3/6 |
| Side Stalls (Front) | ... ... ... | 2/6 |

Members' ballot for tickets on 5th April, 1959
Box Office at Gateway from 6th April, 1959

*A donation from the proceeds will be given to local charities*

*Press review from the Daily Express, April 1959 kindly supplied by Alexander (Alan) Brebner*

# The opera amateurs hit top note

EVERYONE connected with the Edinburgh Opera Company's production at the *Gateway* of Henry Purcell's "Dido and Aeneas" deserves congratulations. These amateurs bring to their work an enthusiasm and sincerity that disarms criticism. The Dido of Miss Dorothy Robertson is a performance of which a professional might feel proud. Her rich voice and splendid acting were at their height in the closing scene of the Queen of Carthage's tragic story.

Alan Brebner as Aeneas, an excellent voice, would have been even more effective if he had thrown restraint to the winds and played with more freedom.

Specially effective were June Geissler's dancers as witches and cupids. Andrew Miller's musical direction of the Edinburgh Chamber Orchestra and the company was excellent, and Mr. Cecil Hole's production had smoothness and some neat touches.

*Dido and Aeneas in performance*

*Dorothy in the front row....*

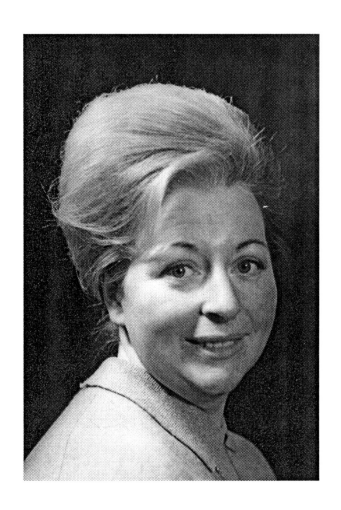

*Scottish Opera publicity shot...*

*Preparing for a role – photograph supplied by May Falconer*

*Shots from Dorothy's youth... on the beach*

*Dorothy and Helen*

*In concert*

*At home in Edinburgh...*

*In a garden…*

*At home again…*

I remember Dorothy…

Janet de Vigne is a publisher, singer and actor. She won the 2003 Leon Sinden award for Best Actress in a Supporting Role during the the Pitlochry Festival Theatre season of that year and will be giving a master class there – in singing - in December 2005.

I remember the first day I met her. I'd come to Edinburgh hoping to be able to get on with some singing and thought that the music library would be the best place to start. I found a gentleman advertising singing coaching there and mentioning quite specifically his Blüthner grand piano. I thought that someone investing so heavily in his art would surely be able to point me in the right direction – when I arrived at his house, I committed the cardinal sin of resting my bag on the piano… and was roundly (and justly) reprimanded! Ian Gilchrist it was who so kindly introduced me to Dorothy, I sang for her at his house and she agreed to take me on. That was in 1991.

Many years later we shared jokes, concerts, the ups and downs of life, sad stories, happy stories and all the great things that grow from a truly rewarding friendship. Being a singer can mean a certain attention to detail after a concert or performance that non-singers usually find intolerable after the first thirty minutes. Dorothy, however, could always be relied upon for an enthusiastic blow by blow technical account of anything we'd seen, together or apart. As going to bed very late was another speciality, you could always pop round for a cuppa at a time when most normal people should be nodding off. Dorothy would have covered the dishes in the sink in the kitchen with a tea cloth, as she was teaching from ten in the morning to ten at night often without a break, but there would be no objection to entertaining into the wee small hours. In fact she would be more likely to insist - a cup of tea or coffee and any amount of tempting confectionery beautifully presented on a tray. You would often be handed an immoral number of ginger biscuits (the best in the world, from the fish man) and told to 'eat up!'

I know for a fact that many of us would present ourselves at her door at some unearthly hour and in some damaged condition. Dorothy was so much more than a teacher. I know her shoulder soaked up more tears in Edinburgh probably than any minister's or barperson's.

Writing a memoir is difficult because you remember things in a non-temporally correct way – pictures flash into your mind as you write, and you don't want to stop for fear of losing them. So bear with me – no dates, but some great stories.

Dorothy and her friend Helen (writer of much in this book) would go to Ireland on holiday every so often, to catch some plays in Dublin or attend short courses on writing in Wicklow, taught by such luminaries as Seamus Heaney (known there as famous Seamus). Once, in a taxi on the way to a theatre, they were treated to a marvellous discourse on the problem of the ozone layer by a wonderfully articulate taxi driver. He said 'Well now, my wife uses the hairspray that they say is part of the problem. I know she's not contributing to it at all – she never uses it outside the house!'

Dorothy married her beloved John on her twenty first birthday. Ken was not her only child – Dorothy had a little girl too whom she lost after a few short days. Dorothy's brother, Drew, and his wife Hilda, lived in Newcastle. A successful chemist, he devised Panadol (as branded by ICI). He was lost to the family before his time, and Dorothy missed him. She really loved her nieces and grandnieces. Dorothy cared for her mother for years after her father died – he had a stomach disorder and was told to eats oats as they were gentle on the system. Dorothy and John built the little extension on their bungalow for her mother, who had her own sitting room, bathroom and bedroom. You would not have wanted Dorothy to brush your hair at any point – she was very hard with the brush and old me once that her mother always used to complain about it. Dorothy's mother was born in Godalming in Surrey and was always elegant and neat about her person, very ladylike and charming.

Dorothy had a boxer dog, tales of him were legion and extraordinary. One day she returned home to discover her new peach coloured marabou feather hat totally demolished and the dog, Macduff, lying on the bed feigning total innocence while peach coloured snow floated gently in a cloud around him - 'it wisnae me' being a particular expression. Dorothy hated hats anyway, she never liked wearing them, saying they didn't suit her. We'll all remember her being beautifully dressed, with real style in the way she chose shapes and colours. She designed and sewed many of her beautiful dresses by hand and had some great secret sources for clothes and accessories which I am not able to disclose!

Dorothy's beautiful grandchildren, Natasha and Chantal, provided an endless fount of inspiration. What a Nana they had in Dorothy – all the cotton reels all over the floor so they could play shops, all sorts of amazing ideas and fun to be had in her treasure trove. Dorothy had two carpets of a similar design in different colours – one pink, in the dining room, one blue in the piano room. One day everything went a bit suspiciously quiet, so Dorothy went into the dining room to find Natasha whispering loudly into her sister's ear: 'You see that?' (pointing to the round design on the carpet) 'That's an elephant's footprint!' A little later, Dorothy heard a little voice squealing in the piano room 'I don't believe it! I don't believe it!' (Chantal was pointing down at the same design but on a blue background) 'He's been in here as well!'

There is a fantastic story about Chantal's first performance as a dancer. She must have been aged about four. Dorothy was identified as the Nana of this beautiful child as she walked into the seating area for the performance 'Oooh – are you that little girl's granny? She was the star of the show last night!' Well, the curtain rose to show a lot of little girls dressed as rosebuds, for their star performance was to unfold, (presumably in the various stages of flowering), do a wee dance and then trip off. Guess who wasn't playing? Uh huh. Chantal sat there glowering at someone in the wings and would not move a muscle. Clearly her teacher spotted the problem and tried to make encouraging noises from off stage. Chantal folded her arms and in a magnificent display of grumpiness turned her back on the audience, by now in gales of laughter. More followed. The little girls exited left – except for Chantal. The curtain came down. The curtain rose again. There was Chantal, arms still folded, back to the audience. Dorothy was practically in hysterics. Later Chantal explained what had happened to Ros: 'Well I'd done it already last night.'

Natasha and Chantal are lovely kids, both very different and both very remarkable people. Dorothy of course used to spoil them rotten – they could stay up as long as they liked when she was baby sitting and used to love spending the night in her house. Chantal - at the age of about four or five - once challenged one of Dorothy's friends. I think the family were in the Botanics and the friend pointed out the squirrels: 'That's not right,' said Chantal 'It's quirrel – when you add an 's' it's plural'. Scary, eh?

Dorothy was a very good photographer. Some may remember the beautiful picture of Natasha and Chantal that was in the piano room; the elder girl leaning over the younger one. It's a picture that captures the sisters perfectly – Natasha, dreamily in touch with the mysterious, Chantal, packed with energy and about to burst into action. That's just reminded me of another couple of Chantal stories: when she was about three or four, Chantal came into Dorothy's house and said 'Can I do something?' Dorothy said 'Of course' wondering what was going to happen. Chantal threw herself on the floor in a fit of what can only be described as Victorian melancholy and cried: 'Ah! I am ruined!!' Dorothy told me she was convinced she'd been here before. A classic instance of what it means to be that age occurred when Chantal, entering Nana's house on another occasion said 'Hi Nana – where are the biscuits?' Ros immediately told her it was very rude to demand biscuits when you go into someone's house, so Chantal said 'All right then – where's the chocolate?'

Dorothy really loved her family and they always came first. At home one Sunday afternoon, Dorothy was in the garden digging the ground. Her hands touched something soft and furry and with a scream she was back inside the house in seconds. Ros (much braver!) went out to see what it was – a fox cub that had clearly died just after birth and been buried probably by its mother in the flowerbed. Ros was great with the kids at this point – she showed them the fox and the little thing was perfectly formed – though I don't think Dorothy wanted to go anywhere near it. Dorothy had had some other interesting experiences with foxes in the back garden – in a soft attempt to scare one away she'd thrown a small pebble at it. The fox picked up the stone, brought it nearer to her, and then went back and sat expectantly waiting for her to throw it again!

Dorothy's family was extremely well connected in the world of the stage – she was related to Dame Anna Neagle (originally Marjorie Robertson) on her father's side and numbered many musicians as well among her relatives. She taught the bel canto method of singing and would never sing to you to try to get over what she meant about a particular technical or musical point, lest you try to copy her. Her understanding of technique was particularly strong and she would explain it in a very non-metaphorical and practical way, talking simply about tongue, facial muscles and above all the soft palate – key components of the instrument sometimes neglected by many singing teachers. Dorothy's own voice was similar I think to the great sound of Elly Ameling but with a true dramatic dimension. I heard her recording of *Exultate Jubilate* once but she would never push herself forward – another sign of a truly gracious human being. I remember her telling me as well that one of her friends was the daughter of TE Lawrence's batman – just another incidence of the rule of 'six degrees of separation'. Voices that she particularly loved include that of Renée Fleming, Magdalena Kozena and Galina Gorchakova. She said that Gorchakova's voice was the sound of the century, so rich and exciting that it reminded her of Callas. It should be remembered that all these singers have gone on to amazing things after successful appearances at the Edinburgh Festival. Dorothy was at the only performance Callas gave at the Festival – complaining of the cold, the diva left before her second concert and ended up meeting Onassis on his yacht. Who knows what might have happened had she stayed and completed her second performance?

Dorothy introduced me to the amazing sound of Florence Foster Jenkins. Well do I remember playing this little 45 rpm single record (remember those??) on the stereo in the spare room. We laughed ourselves stupid! I remember saying 'Why are we bothering? If you can make a great career singing like that...' This good lady's bash at the Queen of the Night is a truly breathtaking experience. Thoroughly recommended to anyone who is feeling low!

Dorothy used to host amazing parties and would feed regularly numbers of more than twenty with great glee. She would hand-make Christmas crackers and decorate her dinner table so beautifully it was a joy to see. I stayed with her more than once during some quite difficult times for us both – I hope I was as great a friend to her as she was to me – and had the privilege of joining the family one year for Christmas. At one party I remember seeing Dorothy and Ken (the son of whom she was so proud) in the kitchen. Ken was explaining something which Dorothy had not fully understood, and I remember hearing him say, in a gently exasperated tone 'It's what I do, Mum!' I had to smile at the incongruity of this – the great doctor (for so you are Ken) just as exasperated as any of us but with a marvellously theatrical mother! (Ken is a doctor working with children in autism. He has such a sense of comfort about him that some children, normally completely incommunicative, will run into his arms when they see him. Dorothy was tremendously proud of this).

Dorothy loved Ros and all her family and what a great bunch they all are. Ros' sister Caroline is a beautiful dancer and Dorothy really admired her work. Ros is a wonderful athlete – she does impossible and frightening things like marathons and the Edinburgh

Triathlon (held every year at New Year in the freezing cold, you run, you swim, you cycle – at least two of these three done in the wet. Pure insanity!) We couch potatoes can only look on in awe and wonder! Dorothy loved to watch athletics on the TV and was also very fond of the golf and snooker.

After Dorothy's funeral Ros' father George turned to me with a smile and said 'She always said I was a crooner!' Dorothy had teased him about this. She was, I remember, amazed at some people's success in the business when they so plainly lacked an instrument. That is no reflection on you, George!

I was particularly grateful to Jenny Logan, Andy Fraser and Gerald McColgan for joining me in the Benedictus from the Mozart *Requiem* at the funeral. It was difficult enough to sing at all, made easier by being able to hide in the organ loft, and they pulled a super performance out of thin air. Dorothy taught Jenny and Gerald but not Andy – they knew each other because every so often we used to pop round very late at night for a wee cuppa either after a gig or some crazy night out. Dorothy liked Andy's pure tenor sound very much; once we went round with his guitar and sang a couple of folk type songs that we used to do for Council of Music in Hospitals gigs. Dorothy had a friend there at the time so they got an impromptu concert, complete with banter – no surprise there. I think they enjoyed it! Andy kept us entertained with stories of hospital performances – such as the lady who greeted one of his songs with the words 'You're rubbish, you stink, I hope you die!'

You would know when Dorothy was 'at home' because the front door was open. She had a lovely little arrangement of plants around the step as well. It took considerable persuading to make her lock the inside door, and eventually the family bought her a wind chime (for security reasons) which made a pleasant tinkling sound whenever anyone came in. Dorothy could not stand a fuss – she was very practical and down to earth about many things – I think this was one of the reasons why she was such a good teacher. This extended to household appliances and her health – she was heroically stoic about these things! I do remember being in the house with Dorothy doing something and hearing Helen saying 'Janet, could you come and help me with this dear?' It didn't sound urgent so I ambled through to the kitchen – and there was Helen with her thumb over the faucet vainly trying to staunch what looked like the jet d'eau on Lake Geneva. 'Oh yes that tap's not right I'll fix it' said Dorothy and lo! It was fixed.

Helen first met Dorothy when she was involved in the Glasgow Grand Opera's production of Macbeth. There's a superb story from this production told by Helen in this book, but suffice it to say that Dorothy's performance was superb. 'There was this very young blonde girl', to paraphrase Helen, 'having a laugh in the corner of the room. Then she came on to sing and she changed – grew six inches taller and took on a completely different aspect, 'eyes flashing fire' – everything appropriate to the character'.

Performers are known for being a bit naughty to each other on stage, particularly if they know the parts well and aren't worrying about the next notes. Dorothy sang with Richard Lewis (whom she described as one of the great British tenors, sadly not as well recognised in his own country as abroad) in *Don Giovanni*. She was Donna Anna to his Don Ottavio. Something was going on, Lewis was a terrible prankster, so to get her revenge Dorothy put a chocolate mint cream in her hand and ever so lovingly rubbed it all the way down his upstage cheek. For the rest of the scene Richard couldn't turn his face to the audience, so he spent a good ten minutes – and one interminable aria - only facing one way. (I could be wrong here and may be confusing Richard with another tenor. Dorothy certainly did know him well, but possibly worked with him on *Cosi fan Tutte* while she understudied Elizabeth Harwood). Geraint Evans was another singer who Dorothy knew and respected tremendously, her respect was returned. She would often quote him on technical aspects of singing.

Unlike some sopranos, Dorothy was a big fan of tenor voices. I say 'unlike' as I have the picture indelibly printed on my mind of the scene where Mario Lanza (as Caruso) arrives late for a rehearsal with a truly celebrated diva. Having thrown a cushion at him, she exclaims in rounded, furious tones 'Tenor is not a voice! It's a disease!!' I suppose tenor jokes for singers are the equivalent of blonde jokes for the rest of you, but I have to say sopranos don't get off lightly there either. In case some of these have escaped you, the all time classic is 'What do you call a field full of sopranos? A vegetable patch!'

Dorothy understudied Elizabeth Harwood in the roles of Donna Anna and I think Fiordiligi, and she rehearsed with Dame Janet Baker (Dorabella) in London. She noted that Ms Harwood was able to appear perfectly coiffed and immaculate at the stage door only ten minutes after a particularly gruelling performance. Dorothy found out why – Elizabeth confided that she kept a selection of neat little wigs for the purpose – it being impossible to sort out under-Mozartian-wig pin-curled hair in anything less than a four hour salon treatment. Pop the wig on over the top and – hey presto!

Diva leaves theatre for her social rounds with nary a hair out of place.

Dorothy enjoyed working with all the singers she knew. On tour she would stay up late playing cards when most of the others had gone to bed – in various stages of disrepair. She was a completely faithful, loving and trusting person. On one tour she sang with a celebrated alto for whom Benjamin Britten had written many roles. Unaware of this lady's sexual preferences, Dorothy accepted an invitation to lie down in her room – just for a wee nap. Emerging totally unscathed she was rather surprised to receive a few odd looks from the company.

Dorothy sang the title role of *Madam Butterfly* to great acclaim, with Ramon Remedios in the role of Pinkerton. Someone whispered to her that her singing in the love duet was creating such a blissful effect in him that the white trousers of his suit needed sent out for cleaning after every performance. Sure enough, observing his dressing room door after the duet, Dorothy spotted the trews on their way to the dry cleaners.

Dorothy was required to paint her chin green for this role. The producer (the word for director in opera, if I may name names I think it was Peter Ebert) had noted her seemingly 'heavy jowl' and apparently green made this disappear on stage. Charming! (But certainly working for me!) Dorothy was greatly admired by Walter Susskind (the famous conductor) as well as singers of such stature as Ian Wallace, Geraint Evans and Richard Lewis.

Dorothy sang the role of the first Rhine Maiden for Sir Alexander Gibson. On stage and without her glasses she was blind as a bat (as was Callas) so she and Sir Alec had this joke going about having a piece of thread tied to her toe which he would pull when she was to come in.

This was never needed – Dorothy's scrupulous attention to detail and focus were legendary. She could (and did) learn a role over night. Strauss songs were a particular favourite (that's Richard rather than Johann) but she also sang the Governess in the *Turn of the Screw*. Some idiot a few years later, hearing that Dorothy had sung this role some twenty years previously, asked her to perform a bit of it there and then. Ridiculous suggestion – you learn a role and then forget it, then go back and learn it again – sometimes it's easier, sometimes not. Dorothy sang too in Britten's *Midsummer Night's Dream* – with Tim Curry (same Tim Curry of *Rocky Horror* fame) playing Puck. Sic transit gloria. Dorothy knew everybody in broadcasting in Scotland and sang as far away as Orkney on many tours.

There's a great story of one of the tours to the islands. Dorothy had flown up to this gig because she'd been doing something else down south; the rest of the singers were coming by car and boat. Well, the snow started coming down thick and fast and the plane couldn't land at the island's airstrip, so the pilot flew as low as he dared over a farmer's field, the farmer who'd been radioed in advance arrived in a truck with a few mattresses in it and Dorothy had to jump out of the plane and land in the truck! After all that she was the only one who'd made it in time for the concert – the bad weather stopped the ferries as well. I do like to think of her jumping out of the plane in full concert kit, high heels and all. It's so very Dorothy!

On another Arts Council trip to the islands Dorothy was singing with the marvellous Edinburgh pianist, Kathleen Belford (the only pupil from the British Isles taken by the great Solomon). They had a very poor turnout for what sounded like a fantastic concert, Wolf,

Strauss etc. and Dorothy went to ask a local chap why they'd had no audience. 'Ah you should have been here last week for the Girls' Brigade gang show' he said, 'the place was packed!' Just at a wee tangent, I have been told by people who know that Kathleen's performance of Rachmaninov's third piano concerto was the finest performance of anything they have ever heard anywhere. It took place at the Usher Hall in Edinburgh and there were queues around the building to get whatever remaining tickets might be obtained.

Dorothy used to lend us all her music – typically generous hearted – and you would often learn so much from her own comments written in a beautifully neat and flowing style. This neatness and precision were present too in her sewing ability – she would often have a skirt, jacket or shirt cut out on the dining room table to be sewed exquisitely by hand once she'd stopped teaching. Dorothy had a few marvellous secrets which I don't suppose she would mind me sharing. One of these at least is the button secret – instantly transform an ordinary cardigan or coat by replacing the buttons with fabulously exciting new ones. Like any true seamstress Dorothy loved trimmings. I brought her back buttons from New York's Sixth Avenue the first time I went – anyone who has been there will know why!

Jane Butters is a lady who has enjoyed some fame in Edinburgh as a painter mostly of botanical subjects. Dorothy went on an art course run by Jane who said she was surprised that Dorothy's work was so big, ebullient and packed with colour. She'd expected it to be tiny and precise. The lavender coloured paintings of flowers in the piano room were Jane's gift to Dorothy.

Dorothy regularly won flower arranging prizes in the local shows with her miniature arrangements - a difficult and very skilled operation - I bet they were absolutely lovely. We know what a great eye for colour she had. I have this idea that where she is now, Dorothy is aware of this book as if almost leaning over my shoulder saying – 'ooh, don't forget that' with a really naughty chuckle!

I used to bring Dorothy wee prezzies from wherever I went, as did many of her pupils. The score in the shape of Cologne cathedral was something I found for her in the 90s when I was living there - I was so pleased she'd liked it enough to frame and put it on the wall. We had a great friend named Jim who used to keep us vastly entertained with outrageous stories of home and abroad; when he left to go and live in France we both missed him but Dorothy would often say it specifically: 'he's such a miss, isn't he?' One of Jim's best (and cleanest) stories was about the 'international trifle'. He had a dear old auntie who, every time he went away on holiday, would provide him with a packet of food to take with him. Upon arrival at his destination Jim would find himself furnished with a jelly, a packet of custard, a very Scottish gold bar and any number of other, more instantly accessible perhaps, delicacies. He would then take it upon himself to find hot water, milk and sugar and make sure that he made a trifle in every place visited. This is probably some kind of record.

We may tend to think that Dorothy didn't travel much outside the UK, but this is not so. Dorothy and John used to travel to Germany, to the Black Forest where they had good friends. (John had served his National Service with the paras). Their friends there were an interesting pair and had been introduced to Dorothy by Kathleen Belford, who often went on holiday together with them. Dorothy loved walking in the Forest.

Dorothy and I managed to get to New York in 2003. I was quite unhappy at this time and still feel I could have made much more of an effort to do things which pleased her. I'd planned a fairly difficult itinerary, but I'd expected Dorothy not to have any problem keeping up – isn't it funny how you expect people to go on and on. I was quite surprised when she couldn't, so of course we slowed down. I only realised later from talking to Ros (Dorothy's beloved daughter in law) that her breathlessness was becoming a bit of a problem. Despite this her sense of humour was still there – she tried for ages to persuade me to climb onto a big digging machine we found lying around in New York somewhere! We went into Tiffany's and really enjoyed looking at the magnificent jewels. We brunched with the best just round the corner from Times Square, went up the Empire State (called Ros and everyone else we could think of from the top on my mobile) and went to two performances at the Met, which was of course the reason for going. On arrival we got to sleep for a couple of hours and then went out to the Barber of Seville. Dorothy slept right through it! (This wasn't unusual unfortunately, it was a particular gift – we often had to subtly nudge her to wake her up in a theatre). On our last day we had lunch on Fifth Avenue and watched a parade, which seemed to go on for ever. On removing our luggage from the hotel to the cab Dorothy had an interesting experience in the reception area – two guys went in and agreed a rate for the room for two hours. Umm, sharp exit. Our taxi to the airport was attacked by a road rage maddened driver who seemed to think he owned the place – at one point I thought he was going to smash the windows, but I had Dorothy securely locked in! We also witnessed a rather spectacular car chase and arrest – the best of NYPD - in

Queens – we'd heard about a man who'd murdered his mother earlier in the week and were fairly hopeful that this was the very man. Getting to the airport slightly late benefited us in this instance – we were upgraded to business class with lovely Aer Lingus (we went with them because I didn't want Dorothy hanging about in the usual customs queue at JFK after such a long flight - the Irish do all the visa stuff before you leave Dublin). We drank champagne and dined on smoked salmon and had an altogether exactly what-we-should-have-been-born-to-experience on the way back. I only wish I could have taken her to La Fenice and La Scala as well – Dorothy would have loved that.

Dorothy had a pupil, a tenor, who although possessed of a lovely instrument, found it incredibly difficult to read music or attain any degree of real musicality. In order to understand how to sing quietly, for example, this chap would crouch down by the leg of her grand piano, and attempt a crescendo as he leapt up. This may not have been one of the strangest things witnessed by Dorothy during many long years of teaching, but it must rank fairly high in the truth versus fiction stakes. One pupil, in her desire not to disturb a lesson but nevertheless deliver some oranges (the question 'why? And why oranges?' has never been fully explained, presumably something to do with vitamin C) rang on the door and crawled into the piano room on all fours. To Dorothy this seemed like a ghostly experience… from where she was sitting, the door appeared to open all by itself and then close again. Very strange. And suddenly there was a pile of oranges under the piano!

Dorothy asked me to do a wee entertainment with her once for a Women's Guild meeting, or some such. Honestly – the way we were treated! We were told rather rudely (after asking politely) that we could throw our coats somewhere; having declined (equally politely) we went on to our performance, Dorothy was playing. After one number we suddenly had everyone's attention – which was just as well, the piano was about a fifth down. We used to have a good laugh about that! Dorothy never prided herself on her piano playing. She told me once that she'd been put forward to play at a school concert, forgot the music a few bars through so went back and just kept playing the bit she could remember... to the polite bemusement of the audience. Dorothy was called on to play in some pretty interesting situations and could always accompany you at the piano even with just the one finger in a lesson. She didn't like her piano very much as it had been a pianola in a previous life and obviously hadn't appreciated the conversion.

Dorothy was a great believer in talent being only one tenth of the necessary in order to get on. Slogging away comprised the rest – you may know the saying: What's the difference between and soprano and a mezzo or a tenor and a baritone? Hard work. She told me how she had to practise this herself – sometimes the voice just would not come, and she would go away and cry for a bit, and then come back to it. Great determination and discipline were the keys. You may ask yourself, 'If Dorothy's talent was so great, why didn't she achieve world recognition and super stardom?' It's a good question, and something that I have learned over the years due in part to her inspiration. Your life is your life – it's up to you to make of it what you will. Sometimes the sacrifices demanded by huge success are simply too much, and will destroy the carefully balanced existence you have built around you and impact too greatly on your nearest and dearest. Dorothy told me that when she'd been asked by Gibson to join Opera for All she had had to refuse – Ken was only two and she just couldn't leave him. She cried herself to sleep that night. Then, the next day someone called from Scottish Opera and said 'Well we want you, so we'll accommodate you. Would you please appear as guest artist for us singing Donna Anna and Butterfly? We'll fly you down as and when'. This I think goes to show that Dorothy made the right decisions, and that life (or God if you like to look at it that way) rewarded her for doing this. She definitely thought she had done the right thing. Matching desire to circumstance is possibly the answer; though please don't think that by saying that I am advocating a lazy or careless approach to life. One can only do what one can do at the time, and there are many, many more things in a truly fulfilled existence than traipsing round the world living out of a suitcase. Dorothy grew older gracefully too, with no regrets and no unmet longing or bitterness in her personality. These are the real achievements of a good life.

Once, when singing a very high profile *Messiah*, Dorothy had the unfortunate experience of seeing someone dry completely. The soloists were placed carefully on little round podia, one each, with a tasteful surround of greenery. The tenor, who shall remain nameless, had decided to do the concert without a score... and dried. No one could help – an excruciating experience for all, but especially the tenor.

One of my last conversations with Dorothy revealed more about her as a human being. She used to walk everywhere until breathlessness became an issue, and on this occasion she had taken the bus up to Princes' Street gardens. Sitting there on a bench with a good book to read, Dorothy got chatting first to a Chinese couple, over on holiday, then a Belgian chap, then a couple of others. She was talking to me later on that day about several of her neighbours of a similar age who were complaining of loneliness. 'I went up to the Gardens and I talked to so many different people – how can anyone say they are lonely when you could go and do that!' I can hear her laughing as she spoke even now, but I do wonder if she was lonely. It's possible of course to be lonely in a room full of people. And can you imagine teaching from ten in the morning to ten every night? Four nights a week?

I think it is very important to remember Dorothy as a human being. People will say 'She never had a bad word to say about anybody' which is true, but she was a person of very strong character and beliefs. I didn't agree with her political views but then, if we all agreed to disagree so lovingly the world would be a better place. If you don't know, perhaps at this point I could just outline what happened to Dorothy before she died.

Dorothy's central heating packed in last winter. She refused to go and stay with Ros and it was very cold last year as I'm sure you remember. Dorothy had a number of electric heaters in the flat so she would snuggle up with these on in the back room. Unfortunately one night, as she was wont to do, she fell asleep in front of the fire and burned her shins very badly. She didn't say a word about it, bandaged up the legs and carried on. (Dorothy was always very heroic about illness – she once broke both her arms at once through falling off a ladder while cleaning the windows. Not a murmur of complaint did she utter). The legs didn't heal – burns being quite tricky to deal with and this not being the way to do it – so she ended up in bed with Ros popping in a lot every day, and a district nurse coming to change the dressings on her shins. (Dorothy didn't like wearing dresses or short skirts – she said she had dumpy legs and would only wear long skirts or trousers). On the day she died, Ros and Ken had collected her from Craigleith and she'd spent the most wonderful day with the family. It was Easter Sunday, a beautiful day and the first time she'd been out of the house for ages. We were all hoping of course that we'd be able to start lessons again in the summer term – it was not to be. Dorothy told Ken and Ros that she wasn't feeling well and Ros asked if she'd like to go home. The answer was 'yes' and Dorothy had just stood up and was walking to the door when she collapsed and was rushed to hospital. It was a heart attack. Although we miss her dreadfully and wish that this hadn't happened, if she had to go at all this was a lovely way to do it, surrounded by her nearest and dearest and in the blazing sunshine of a gorgeous Edinburgh day.

I was away from Edinburgh when I heard the news. It took a while for reality to set in again – not exactly sure that it has, really, yet, especially with having just had the first Festival without her. I was very grateful that I was allowed to see Dorothy at the funeral home the day before the church service; I had been thinking about going, but a very dear friend (thank you) came with me and it really calmed me down somehow – Dorothy looked as though she was just asleep, as if a dream was occupying her mind. I held that image of her dear face as we sang the Benedictus. I don't think I could have managed Panis Angelicus unless I had seen her. It became an intensely intimate emotional experience, singing over her in that way.

I heard a fantastic story about Dorothy at her funeral. A friend who had known Dorothy from the age of three told us he had invited her out to sing at a concert for which he was playing the organ, when she was seventeen. Dorothy was all dolled up in a gorgeous posh frock, hair perfect and this chap arrived at the door... on a bicycle. I don't know if she made it to the concert balanced on the handlebars or riding side-saddle on the back. Dorothy had told me another story too – some famous opera producer had arrived at her parents' house for high tea. The gentleman was in full flood extolling her virtues, her warm and friendly personality and her rounded tones (possibly some hint of a rounded person in here too). Dorothy's father, presumably delighted to hear his daughter praised so highly, chipped in with 'Yes, she's always been a happy little butter ball!' Nothing like relying on your parents to keep up the glamorous mystique of the profession, eh?

I know we will all remember Dorothy with great affection. There are thousands of other stories about her that won't feature in this book. I really hope though that in reading this hearts will be warmed and that we'll be encouraged to carry on as she did. Dorothy never complained, was always there for you – had a heart of gold and a talent to match. She was generous in spirit and gesture, never gave in to snobbery (was sometimes amused, sometimes frustrated by it) and loved all forms of the performing arts. How sorely we will miss her, remember how much we loved her, and feel our hearts warmed by the certainty that where she is, she is smiling at us. The words of Peggy Ashcroft describing Molly Urquhart could, as Helen has said, easily describe our Dorothy: 'She was like sunshine entering a room'.

# Anecdotes and Tributes

With fondest love…

A few years ago I was in Dublin and I borrowed Dorothy's raincoat for a few hours. It was stylish, lightweight and eminently packable – and has been my Holy Grail of raincoats ever since. The incident provides a useful peg on which to hang not the coat but some reflections of Dorothy herself.

Her warm support of others for instance: she was in Dublin to support Janet (singing in the Anna Livia Opera Festival); her genuine interest in and benevolent influence on the lives and careers of those she knew were exceptional. I cannot recall any chance encounter, however inconvenient the occasion, which did not leave me with the uplifting glow of certainty that I had just made Dorothy's day – whereas in fact it was she who had just made mine!

The flair for style which made that raincoat such a glorious garment extended beyond personal appearance – perhaps her stage training gave Dorothy the inspiration to set up her teaching room so harmoniously, to just the right mixture of prettiness and sense of occasion. That the flowers on the piano were usually a present from a pupil was a clear sign of how much she was valued.

There is plenty more to say about Dorothy and each of us will have our own memories of the sight, sound, humour and charm of her – a private essence to take out and uncork from time to time. For myself I'd like to thank her for far more than the loan of a raincoat, and bid her my goodbye in her own words 'with fondest love'.

Katharine Wake, flautist and pupil

An extraordinary person...

Dorothy was a superb teacher and a delightful person. I was a 'mature student' having had my initial training with others, but I found her to be inspirational and of tremendous help.

Kathleen Patrick, friend and pupil

She was just such an encouragement I wish I had found her thirty years before!

Mary Gordon, pupil

Happily helping an amateur voice enjoy lessons...

I was first introduced to Dorothy by another pupil of hers and a good friend of mine: Jeannie Wheater. My family had said to me quite categorically:

'Either learn to sing properly before you get any older and it's too late... or give up now!'

You know the sort of advice one is given by one's nearest and dearest... So, after a phone call to arrange an audition, with great trepidation I arrived at Dorothy's. Practical, down to earth and enthusiastic as always, she asked me to sing something. This I just managed to do (with my knees knocking) and to my great relief, she said

'We can easily do something with your voice!'

So I was much relieved and have enjoyed five years of happy hours learning new music and learning how to use my voice and diaphragm purely for my own pleasure.

I am a mere amateur among her bevy of distinguished pupils but she treated me just the same, put up with my frequent business travel absences and my evident lack of practice. And most of all, she taught me to sing in my late 50s and made the learning of new works so enjoyable even when the language was impenetrable and the melodic lines challenging. Dorothy had the wonderful attributes of enthusiasm, kindliness and encouragement, so that even my worst efforts were looked on positively. As a result I always felt exhilarated and enthused after an hour's lesson, in fact it never seemed like a lesson but a wonderful enjoyment of making music together: she as a superb pianist and accompanist and me doing my best to please her and to enjoy myself.

It has been a rare privilege to have been one of Dorothy's pupils and something I shall treasure all of my days.

Roger Crofts, pupil

The 'spot Dorothy' competition...

A fond memory of myself, Anne O'Reagan and Lyn Jones – all pupils of Dorothy and also second sopranos in the Edinburgh Festival Chorus...

Dorothy came to all our concerts, and the three of us had a 'competition' at each one to see who would spot Dorothy first, after we filed onto the platform. We are not allowed to speak once we're on the platform, but we became experts in communicating without moving our lips!! As you can imagine, this Festival has been sad for us in not seeing Dorothy there. A couple of times I found myself looking for her, before remembering that she couldn't be there this year.

Avoney Ogilvie, pupil

Thanks for the memories...

I had voice and memory problems after a car accident which happened three and a half years ago. I met Dorothy as my sister, Christine, had begun lessons. I 'do' voices and sing and had been working up to writing a one woman show before the accident. I was extremely upset afterwards to find I couldn't sing for a long time. I had lost my top notes (could sing $A^b$ above top C before). Dorothy reassured me that the voice (a muscle) would come back. Most encouraging of all, she said she would help me with my one woman show. Having lost all my confidence Dorothy made me feel that maybe I did have talent, if she were so willing to help.

We laughed a lot - I described my appearance as a pink confectioner in Half A Sixpence as 'not so much a house end more a small bungalow' and she found that funny.

She told us stories about learning a whole part overnight to take over a leading role in London.

She gave endlessly – 'this would suit your voice Kate ...'

She taped piano accompaniments for me and ignored my woeful ignorance, saying instead 'perhaps you're not familiar with this one, Kate...'

Dorothy was the person/ teacher you meet once in your life.

Kate Hamilton, pupil

A tin ear and the utmost charm…

I've been thinking about times with Dorothy, and can recall many instances when she revealed her tremendous kindness and concern for others. There seemed to be a constant stream of people who would reveal their anxieties and upsets to her, and she always supplied a compassionate and sympathetic hand/shoulder.

Connected to her actual teaching, though, she did help out the son of a friend of mine, a boy completely unknown to her. This was someone who had decided he wanted to be an actor more than anything, and in order to get into LAMDA, he had to do some singing as part of his audition. A completely unmusical boy, from a totally unmusical family, this was causing some worry. Unperturbed, Dorothy selected the piece (Miss Otis Regrets), commented to me in passing that he really did have a tin ear (only much more politely), coached him for a few weeks and sent him off to London saying he had made very good progress. He got in, and he and his family were delighted, not to mention amazed.

This displays, I think, her quiet but extremely focused ambition for her pupils to do as well as possible. All done, as I think you will agree, with the utmost charm.

Nicky Woods, pupil

Lashings of joie de vivre...

On 8 January 1990, I plucked up the courage to ring a singing teacher called Dorothy Robertson. I had been having problems with my singing voice – in fact, I'd lost it completely and, after a consultation at the ERI I was advised to take some singing lessons to try to bring it back to life. From the moment the voice at the end of the telephone trilled: three-three-two four-three-one-nine I could feel the corners of my mouth turning up; nevertheless it was with some trepidation that I turned up in Craigleith for my first lesson.

I couldn't produce any kind of sound, but Dorothy quickly diagnosed the problem ad prescribed a series of exercises to 'raise the soft palate'. After a few weeks of throat warblings, sounds did begin to emerge and Dorothy deemed it time to attack a real song! I shall never forget the title – Bois Epais (Sombre Wood) by Lully. It was indeed sombre. I croaked and gasped my way through to the end and when I arrived 'je ne veux plus souffrir' suffering was certainly the name of the game for the singer and accompanist! I turned to her in anguish and shaking my head mournfully said 'that was just terrible, Dorothy!' At the piano she sat calmly, smiled serenely and said, 'Now now, there were some good things there.' At that moment I knew I had struck gold with this wonderful lady, who dispensed advice and encouragement in such a delightfully charming way.

My voice did improve and more and more 'good things' began to happen so that, after a term, my singing voice was back and I quite thought that would be the end of my singing lessons. Not a bit of it! 'Now' said Dorothy gleefully, 'now we can have some fun!' And fun we had, cantering through the mezzo repertoire with varying degrees of accuracy and musicality on my part but always with lashings of joie de vivre!

By now Dorothy was a firm friend – we laughed our way through Monday lunchtime lessons – through recording sessions making tapes for my grandchildren when Dorothy had to sit on three cushions to reach an extremely unstable keyboard – through happy parties and leisurely lunches. Yes, in the fifteen years I was privileged to know Dorothy there were indeed many, many good things, and a monumental amount of fun!

Irene Smith, pupil

Teaching Mother Goose...

I met Dorothy in around 1996 through her very dear friend, Helen Murdoch. As actor, I was never particularly musical, in fact – I have limited musical ability. Knowing that I was doing pantomime in Kilmarnock, Helen suggested that I give Dorothy a call with a view to working on a panto number.

I went for a few lessons but it wasn't until 2003 that I felt I really needed to do some serious work on my singing. I was engaged to play my first Dame in *Mother Goose* at the Gaiety Theatre in Ayr and was asked if I might manage a couple of songs – 'Friends', made famous in the 1950s by Jack Hulbert and Cicely Courtneidge and 'I am what I am' from the musical *La Cage aux Folles*. Dorothy was eager to get started, inspiring confidence and simplifying the task – 'Friends' became 'Friends, two, three, four, isn't it rather nice to have friends?' She recalled seeing Harry Gordon as a Dame, counting out the beat as he moved so sublimely in his twin set and pearls.

Remembering my first visit to Dorothy's house I arrived slightly early clutching the sheet music of 'Hey look me over', thinking it would make a good opening number for a Dame. Dorothy asked me politely to take a seat in the hall while she concluded the lesson with her previous pupil. On hearing the magnificent soprano voice coming from the room I thought 'Oh dear, should I leave now?'

I need not have worried. Dorothy seemed to enjoy our sessions, taking a keen interest in my work and encouraging me to perform the songs together with the accompanying Mother Goose dialogue which always raised a smile. My debut Dame was warmly received, to my utter surprise, Mother Goose's emergence from the Pool of Youth in a blue sequinned dress, blue powder wig and Dame Edna glasses singing 'I am what I am' became a highlight of the show.

Though Dorothy never managed to come to Ayr, she sent me the most beautiful handcrafted gosling to wish me luck. That little goose still sits in the hallway of my flat today. I perhaps may have seemed a most unlikely pupil but I remain indebted to Dorothy for inspiring confidence in my singing.

Graham Macgregor, pupil and actor

Graham trained as an actor at Queen Margaret University College, Edinburgh. Since 1989 he has appeared regularly in Scottish television and theatre, including sixteen consecutive pantomime seasons. This year he plays Wishee Washee in Aladdin at Motherwell Civic Theatre.

# Photographs – the later years

*The singer on the rock*

*Reading on holiday*

*On holiday again*

*Dorothy and the girls...*
*Back row L-R Blanche, Frances,*
*front row L-R Dorothy, Muriel, Chris, Margaret*

*Prague, taken by Helen Murdoch*

*New York 2003, taken by Janet de Vigne*

Haddington 2003

# End word: Ian Wallace

*What roles have you found to be most demanding, dramatically?*

I think I would single out two. The first was one I sang in Glasgow in 1951. The Glasgow Grand Opera Society were presenting as part of their Festival of Britain *Mefistofele* by Boito. Boito ws Verdi's librettist, a very modest man who composed in secret. They invited two guest singers, Richard Lewis, who was to sing Faust and myself to sing Mefistofele. That was immensely challenging, largely because it was the first time somebody had offered me a serious bass part instead of a comic one. Physically I am not really ideal casting as the Devil, and my personality is probably a little too genial, so it was quite a challenge.

It was an exciting experience and the music was very exhilarating. The Glasgow Grand Opera Society with their huge choru,s were a marvellous group to work with. The other problem for me was that because I am not a true bass I had to darken my voice to try to get the appropriate effect for Mefistofele. I think that affected my diction. Certainly the critic of the Times thought it did and I was inclined to agree with him. That production was memorable for me because the then amateur Scottish soprano, Dorothy Robertson, sang so superbly as Marguerite that, on the first night after her aria, Walter Susskind, who was conducting, put down his baton and joined the audience in applauding her.

From Ian Wallace, a special interview by Helen Murdoch
*Scottish Theatre News*, October 1981, used with permission.

# The obituary

Dorothy Robertson-Aitken was one of the most remarkable singers and teachers of her generation. Dorothy Robertson, as she was known professionally, was a music teacher who, in answer to the old aphorism could not only 'teach' but 'do'. Her singing lessons reflected her own artistry and experience, and she offered practical solutions to the problems and challenges a singer meets. She helped launch many a student well equipped into the world of music.

Born and brought up in Glasgow, Dorothy showed an early talent that was nurtured by her parents, who sent her to elocution and music lessons. Her church in King's Park had a keen organist, Mr Molloy, who had a huge choir for services and concerts. His inspiration helped and encouraged Dorothy, who, with her friend May Falconer, began to sweep the board at local music festival competitions.

Her teachers at King's Park School, one of whom, Helen Reid, was a cousin of Mary Garden, Aberdeen's celebrated opera star, singled her out for solo work and she won a bursary to receive to receive tuition at Glasgow's Athenaeum with James Reid. She enjoyed further success in the British Commonwealth's Best Soprano competition, in which she was placed second.

Joining the Glasgow Grand Opera Society in her late teens, while she was working by day in the Norwich Union, was a major step. This fine society gave full-scale productions with the Scottish Opera and guest directors and singers. Dorothy began to undertake leads; Marguerite in Boito's *Mefistofele*, Lady Macbeth in Verdi's *Macbetto*, and superbly, Lucia in Donizetti's *Lucia di Lammermoor*. Guest male artists included Richard Lewis and Ian Wallace, the latter being particularly impressed by Dorothy, who he was sure would succeed in

London. Similarly the conductors Walter Susskind and Colin Davis, as well as director Peter Ebert, all offered her the chance of a start at Covent Garden.

However Dorothy decided to remain in Scotland. She had met John Aitken, with whom she shared a very happy marriage from 1952 until his untimely death in 1994.

With Scottish Opera she made some guest appearances on the company's touring schedule, as Donna Anna in Mozart's *Don Giovanni* and as a much-praised *Madama Butterfly* (Puccini). She was typically single-minded in her preparations, always making sure she was word and music-perfect, and organising a complete housekeeping schedule for her husband and young son, Kenneth, who offered salient comments on his mother's practising, such as: 'There's that old Lady Macbeth, yelling again'.

Asked to understudy for the main season, she was called early to sing Mistress Ford in Verdi's *Falstaff*, covering for the soprano from Cologne, who could not manage the first rehearsal week. She arrived with the whole part memorised. She considered the privilege of singing with Sir Geraint Evans one of her proudest moments. The company considered itself blessed by its 'understudy'.

Similarly she covered Elizabeth Harwood as Fiordiligi (*Cosi fan Tutte*) Joan Carlyle as Desdemona (*Otello*) which she sang, beautifully while Miss Carlyle mimed for the dress rehearsal, and Catherine Wilson as the Governess in Britten's *Turn of the Screw*. Song recitals on the radio as well as solos with the full Scottish Radio Orchestra kept her in demand, as did her guest appearances with choral societies including Haddo House, Anstruther and the Edinburgh Bach Choir.

A happy partnership with Edinburgh pianist Kathleen Belford – the only British pupil ever trained by the great Solomon – gave numerous arts societies from Shetland to the Borders song and opera recitals of a range and quality that were enjoyed by people who never got to see full versions.

One further chance operatically came when Alex Gibson conducted the first *Rheingold* (Wagner) where Dorothy Robertson, as the first Rhine maiden, sang those thrilling phrases that open the first act.

In recent years, Dorothy found a way to use her music to help young singers and her granddaughters, Natasha and Chantal, whom she encouraged to follow in her footsteps. In her own home, she taught ten hours a day from Monday to Thursday, giving lessons to school pupils, college students, young singers just starting out on their careers, established professional singers and a whole variety of wind instrument players, who found her carefully evolved breathing and voice production techniques invaluable.

Conscious of the struggle young people had, she gave her considerable experience at a modest fee, or sometimes for no fee at all. She also encouraged, listened compassionately, comforted and generally supported with her sunny personality all of them in a way that supplemented their musical acquisition.

Dorothy was a special person, and it was a privilege to know her. Wherever she is, there will be music, love, laughter and understanding.

# Thanks

Thanks are due to the many friends and pupils who submitted material for this book, and also to Ken and Ros Aitken for many of the photographs.

The publisher would particularly like to thank the office of M.J Brown Son & Co, Joan, Barbara R, Nan, Janice, Patricia, Barbara P, Margaret and Amy for coffee, tea, biscuits, barking (that's just Amy) and all their help in putting both the memorial concert and this book together.

Thank you as well to Helen Hutcheson for the line drawings, Stuart Johnston of Zeticula for the layout and Heather Macpherson for the cover, while not forgetting the invaluable contribution of Helen Murdoch.

# Acknowledgements

Permission to reproduce the photographs from the web and the *Evening Post* has been sought by the publisher.

Every effort has been made to trace copyright holders. The publisher will be delighted to correct any error or omission in future editions – please let us know.

All photographs were submitted in their original condition. We have tried to scan them in using the most up to date equipment available, but the quality of some of the prints has not been the best. We hope you will still enjoy and appreciate them.

Lightning Source UK Ltd.
Milton Keynes UK
UKOW02f2022200315

248265UK00001B/69/P

9 781905 565009